Separation, Divorce, and Survival: The Crucial First Seventy Two Hours

BY: Robert W. Rushing, Jr., Esq.

2013 Wilberforce Press

Chapter One

Fasten Your Seat Belt

Too often, in the chaotic time following a separation, an individual makes crucial mistakes that affect him or her for years afterwards. This is hardly surprising. Few people are cold and detached enough to strategize and plan for the difficult process which lies ahead. Still, it is important to try. Just consider the things that can be at risk:

1. Child custody and visitation rights;

2. Possession of property;

3. Division of debts;

4. Attorney's fees and costs;

5. Personal and professional reputation;

6. Personal freedom and safety;

7. Alimony and support.

Thought you may be in more of a mood to cry, you must act. The separation of a married couple, especially with years invested in the relationship, is like an explosion. The repercussions of the even must be anticipated and accounted for in order to control the damage.

Skeptical? Here are a few horror stories to make my point. Several years ago, a man I represented decided to clear the air about a past affair, something he thought would improve his marriage. While his intentions were honorable, the effect was catastrophic.

When he appeared at my office, he had long scratches on both cheeks, and a deep bruise on his right forearm. This, he explained, happened when he decided to come clean about the affair he had years ago. His wife was drinking at the time, which probably should have indicated to him that this not a good time for what he had planned.

He sat down, poured himself one, and spilled his guts. Her first reaction was to go at his face like a wildcat. After he threw her off, she hurled several heavy objects at him, and headed out the door cursing. The last he saw or heard of her for the rest of the weekend was the screech of tires headed out the driveway.

`A couple of days later, he got a call from his credit card company. It seemed they were suspicious of some recent activity regarding his account. About seventy five thousand dollars had been charged to the account over the weekend from various locations up and down the interstate.

Our guy, unfortunately, did not make the kind of money that would have allowed him to take such a financial hit lightly. Worse, because it was a joint account, his wife's vengeful spending spree was all completely legitimate. He had no legal basis to challenge the charges.

He would get some financial relief when the debt was divided pursuant to the divorce decree, but that would be months later. All he could do for the time being was to go to the yellow pages and look for first, a skin specialist, and secondly, a good, aggressive divorce lawyer.

Another client of mine could top this horror story. She had decided, after a long period of attempting to work on the marriage, to tell her husband that she wanted a divorce. The announcement, however, was poorly timed, as it was right before she was to leave on a seven day business trip out of state.

Her husband had no family ties where they resided, having been born and raised in Alaska. Not surprisingly, he developed an urge to go North over the weekend. When she returned home, the house had been cleaned out, and her husband and child were gone without a trace.

She did not have the address, telephone number, or even proper names of her seldom seen in- laws. In fact, other than an educated guess that her husband would return to the state of his birth, she had no clue where he had taken her child. Worse, she soon learned that because there was no custody order, he was within his rights to take the child. She would have to file a petition in family court, locate him, and serve him with the papers, to have a hope of getting her child back.

The story had a happy ending, but only after weeks of sleepless nights, and thousands of dollars spent on attorneys and detectives. This angst and expense all could have been avoided by simply timing the announcement differently, and arranging to take immediate legal action to secure custody of the child.

Events at the end of a marriage are ruled by emotion. For most people, it is highly difficult to sit down and create a rational plan to secure offspring, property, and finances. Nevertheless, the benefits of doing so are incalculable.

If you feel that such an approach is cold, calculated, and insensitive to the other party, ask yourself this question? Will their peace of mind be benefitted in any way by confused, erratic behavior on your part which will make the situation that much more unstable? Would they, in the alternative, benefit by a consistent, respectful, and compassionate approach which minimizes the hurt and conserves resources which will be needed now more than ever?

The truth is that the emotions involved in separation and divorce are not pleasant, unless you count the feeling of relief. All that can be done is to deal with the issues in a way that minimizes the emotional and financial pain to all involved. Any other approach is simply destructive.

CHAPTER TWO: PLAN FOR THE WORST/HOPE FOR THE BEST

Priority one is to establish personal safety for yourself and your family. The first question is one which people tend to shrug off with little though, but should consider more carefully. "Is there any immediate possibility of physical danger to me or my family?" Even in the darkest moments, most of us maintain a certain level of trust for people we care deeply for, and whom we have great emotional investment. The comforting effect of this can distort what should be obvious signs of trouble.

Instead, ask yourself these questions:

1. Have I ever been threatened with physical harm by my spouse?

2. Have I been physically injured by my spouse?

3. Have I ever been mentally abused by my spouse?

4. Does my spouse have a problem with alcohol or drugs? Has this become worse as a result of the marital problems?

5. Does my spouse have a criminal record related to physical violence or substance abuse?

5. Has my spouse ever engaged in stalking behavior? Most of us are clear today on the definition of this term, but in general, if there has been phone, text, and e -mail, or personal communication that frightened you, and which persisted after you asked for it to stop, that would qualify.

If the answer to any of these questions is yes, there are things you must do immediately. Get a recent photograph of him or her, and make plenty of copies. These should be distributed to anyone who might be in the position to safeguard you from harm at some point.

Obvious examples would be your employer, security officers at your business or home premises, and school officials at any school that you or your children may attend. Attach a letter explaining the circumstances, and providing all relevant contact information for yourself and family members.

Depending on the circumstances, it might be wise to send the letter certified or registered mail. The fact that you possess proof that the information is in the hands of an entity intended to receive it is often a strong motivator for them to take your situation seriously.

As difficult as it may be, you also have to examine the real possibility that you or your family are in danger. This is a judgment call that only you, or those closest to you, can make. However, far too many people have given the benefit of the doubt to a person once loved and trusted, with tragic results.

If you have any doubts as to your safety, file for a restraining order. I have had clients explain that they were reluctant to do this, for fear of angering their spouse. They are essentially saying that they are too afraid to seek protection, which makes no sense.

If you obtain a restraining order, provide copies to the same people to whom you would provide copies of the photograph and letter, and get proof that it was received. Keep in mind that a restraining order is little or no protection in and of itself. It is merely a tool that makes it easier for law enforcement to act, AFTER an incident of violence.

Basically, the restraining order works to the extent that it the person being restrained allows it to be. For this reason, the unfortunate truth is that the more irrational, unpredictable, and dangerous the person you seek protection from, the less effective the restraining order will be. For this reason, I always remind my clients that the order does not mean that they are "safe". It is merely a tool in their arsenal that might be used to protect them.

If you are the victim of an act of violence, call law enforcement immediately. If you have been physically injured, go to a doctor you trust immediately. Be sure to obtain a copy of all medical records and bills related to your treatment. If you have bruises, scratches, or marks, photograph or videotape the injured areas before the evidence can fade.

If other parties witnessed all or part of the incident, ask them to write down their recollections in their own handwriting, sign it, and provide you a copy. An e-mail or computer document is helpful, but unlike those, a handwritten, signed statement is in and of itself authentic proof that the witness said certain things. This can be very useful later on, should the witness be reluctant to testify and come up with a sudden case of amnesia.

It is also important to consider your social networks on-line. Nothing is more public than sites like Face book or MySpace, and posting photographs or personal information on these sites is not much different than renting a billboard. If you are involved in an ugly divorce, strongly consider removing yourself from such sites for awhile. If you are addicted, and cannot make yourself do so, at least refrain from constantly posting your whereabouts and day to day activities. This is the first place that a disgruntled, estranged spouse or his or her divorce lawyer, will check for information.

A secondary, but still important, consideration is the securing of personal property. I always suggest that my client take a piece of paper, and make a list with four subsections. The first list of items should include things of great financial or sentimental value to him or her, the "I can't live without it" column.

The second list should be items of less importance or value, but which he or she considers to be uniquely his own. There could be several reasons for this. The item could have been a gift or part of an inheritance. It could be something which, by its nature, could only be used by that person. Most commonly, this includes items used exclusively by, paid for, and maintained by them, such as a car.

The third column should include items that would be considered marital property. In other words, both have equal claim to these items and they are more or less up for grabs. I refer to this as the "red" column since these are the items of property that will be in dispute.

The final column, of course, would be items that are considered to belong to the spouse. These are things that the client does not want, unless or course he needs to recover them to pay an attached debt, as in the case of a wedding ring, or is simply looking to raise funds.

As to the items in the first column, remove them to a secure place outside of the marital home as soon as this can be done safely. One of the most common methods of lashing out at a husband or wife during the breakdown of the relationship is to steal, damage, or destroy their favorite things. I once had a client who had received a purple heart for his brave service in World War II. His second wife took it with her when she left him, and according to her deposition testimony, sold it to a pawn shop for a few dollars in a town whose name she conveniently did not remember. The trial Judge frowned on this spiteful and selfish act, but that did not restore the medal he had planned to leave to his grandchild.

As to the items in the second and third columns, the advice is essentially the same. However, keep in mind that there might be some differing opinions as to who owns what, and under most circumstances, it is better to communicate about the division of the marital property. Many ugly, expensive, and prolonged divorce cases were set off by the spark of a dispute over some trinket of nominal value. Always calculate cost based upon replacement value, and try not to get caught up in the need to "win," when dividing up easily replaceable personal property.

As to the fourth column, if you are in possession of items that clearly belong to your spouse, pack them up carefully, photograph them to prove they are in good condition, and return them upon request. This is said with two words of caution. First of all, be sure to document the good condition of the property with photographs or video, and if possible, the process of your husband or wife recovering the items. The best way to do this is to simply have them sign and date a list of the items they have received, and note on the page that the items were in good condition. Secondly, recognize that it is not necessarily safe to meet with your spouse for this purpose on your own.

Finally, take action to protect your finances and credit rating. Unless the level of trust is exceptionally high, cancel all joint credit cards. Even in the best of circumstances, the high level of tension and probable lack communication between the parties makes this an accident waiting to happen.

Consider doing the same as to joint bank accounts. It is usually not the best idea, ethics aside, to simply rush to the bank, withdraw the money, and close the account. Calculate as accurately as possible the amount of the outstanding checks, and leave a reasonable margin in the account. Then and only then withdraw a reasonable amount based upon needs and the overall situation.

It is difficult to provide a guideline as to just what percentage of the funds should be left in the account. The balance is somewhere between the point at which an opposing attorney can use your actions as a weapon against you in trial, and the point at which you are depriving yourself of your hard earned money. Alternately, twice the total amount of the outstanding checks is a good guideline, provided that any and all affected parties are notified immediately.

If you have children, you now must make the most important decision of all. Technically, child custody is an issue that can be raised in court anytime, and can always be litigated again until the child reaches the age of majority-eighteen in most states. However, in reality, inertia is the dominant factor in child custody cases. In other words, whichever parent get custody and control of the child initially is likely to retain that control for the long haul.

This means that you need to decide now just what relationship you want with your children and your estranged spouse as to raising them. This is obviously a question with no easy answers. Instead, you are to choose the best alternatives of which none are entirely appealing to you. Again, it is impossible to give specific advice without knowing the facts of a situation, but here is my hierarchy of factors which should be weighted in the decision.

1. Is the other parent a danger to the children(ren) due to an abusive personality, drug dependency, or other issue?

2. Is the other parent embittered to such an extent that he or she will attempt to alienate you from your child(ren)?

3. Does the other parent have strong ties to a distant state or nation, such that it is likely that he or she will leave the area and make access to your child(ren) difficult or impossible?

4. Does your child(ren) seem psychologically stable, and relatively accepting of the pending separation of his or her parents? Do you feel adequately informed as to how a prolonged and difficult custody action might negatively affect him or her?

5. Are you and your spouse still able to communicate and cooperate in the best interests of your child(ren), in spite of whatever other difficulties you might have?

6. If you are employed, what effect would taking on full time care giving of your child(ren) have as to your work? Is your employer able and willing to facilitate this with a flexible work schedule, day care services, or other such benefits?

7. Do you have family members who would consistently and reliably assist you in caring for a child(ren) if you were to obtain full time custody?

8. Do you know and are you confident of your child(ren)'s preference of where he or she would want to live? It should be mentioned that answering this question involves a great deal more than just asking the child. Typically, a child will be wary of alienating either parent, and will simply answer such questions by telling that parent what he or she wants to hear. To begin to get a sense of what the child truly wants, assure the child that he is she is not being asked to choose one parent to the exclusion of the other, but rather is being asked for input as to decisions that will affect his life.

9. Who has been the primary caregiver of the child(ren) up to now? Do either you or your spouse have any special skills or knowledge that would be necessary to protect and care for the child(ren)?

10. Can you afford the attorney's fees and expenses involved in a contested child custody case?

If the answer to the first question is yes, you must file for custody. While it is beyond the scope of this book to examine the entire process, aggressively seek out and recruit the best family court lawyer available. Begin to collect the information necessary to convince the court that your spouse is a danger to the child(ren), and secure this information in a place in which he or she cannot find it or destroy it.

If you anticipate that your spouse will accuse you of also not being a competent parent, use sources such as pediatricians, school officials, friends and neighbors to prove that this is untrue. If you have personal problems which you know will concern a judge, seek out whatever help is available to you immediately so that your initiative and improvement can be testified to in court.

The second and third concerns would lead you to strongly consider filing for custody. They indicate a possibility that if you do not retain control, you will lose your relationship with the child(ren). You must evaluate for yourself how real the threat is.

A professional can best answer the fourth question. However, you probably know your own child(ren) far better than any counselor or psychologist, even if the child(ren) is/are already receiving treatment. Try to spend some time talking to the child about the situation. Always assure the child(ren) that your support and love are unconditional, but explain the nature of the decisions that have to be made. With time, you should obtain a better understanding of his or her wants, concerns, and needs.

The patience and selflessness this requires can be difficult to muster. However, any other attitude is certain to be harmful to the child(ren) and lead to a less than honest response. Usually, faced with a blunt "choose one of us" ultimatum, the child(ren) will understandably attempt to placate both parents by telling them what they want to hear, unwittingly making the relationship between the parents even worse due to the miscommunication.

If you can answer the first four questions without deciding that you have to file for custody, your relationship with the child(ren) can remain intact with or without sole custody. The question becomes one of adequate, better, or best care. Keep in mind that joint custody orders are increasingly common in most states, meaning that if the parties are willing to work together, there may be no need for a "winner" and a "loser."

Also, visitation can usually be structured so that the non custodial parent will receive almost as much quality time with the child(ren) as the custodial parent. I have pointed out to many parents that alternating weekends, extended time during the summer, and divided time during major holidays covers about half the time that a custodial parent would have to devote to interacting with the child(ren). In fact, many children I have spoken to claim that they have better access to the non custodial parent after the separation, simply due to a natural change in priorities.

If you are sure that you will be filing for sole custody, do not leave the child(ren) initially in the care of your spouse. This greatly decreases the chance that you will be able to win an initial custody hearing. However, and this is crucial, be aware of the terms of any court order that has already been issued effecting you and the children. If your spouse is already the beneficiary of a child custody order, a violation of that order could be punishable by fine or imprisonment.

One far too frequent family court horror story is that of the non custodial parent who has verbal consent for a visit, and then is astounded when the custodial parent calls the police, resulting in arrest. In such cases, unless there is written proof of the consent of the custodial parent, that parent literally holds the keys to the jailhouse door. There can be no more powerful leverage in a contested divorce action.

Assuming that there is no such order, you should immediately seek one granting you temporary custody of the minor child(ren). Until such an order exists, both you and your spouse are his or her natural custodians, making possession the only law of the case. In other words, if your spouse picks up the child from school and boards and airplane to whereabouts unknown, this is perfectly within his or her rights. Your only option would be to attempt to locate them and serve papers seeking relief from the court. This happens far more often than should be the case.

Whether you leave the marital home or not, it is a good idea to review the household bills and see that everything is paid. There will be inevitable confusion during this period, and it is easy to miss a payment on something important. Even if you anticipate an ugly, prolonged divorce process, few things boost credibility with a judge more than leaving in a considerate, orderly fashion.

Also, if you are leaving, consider writing a note to your spouse. This should be done with considerable thought and care. Avoid any expression of anger or hostility, and any threatening language. However, there is a considerable benefit to documenting the reasons you are leaving at that time, in words of your choosing.

Keep a copy of the letter. Judges typically find such evidence extremely persuasive as to explaining why a couple ceased cohabiting, which in turn has everything to do with the end financial result of a contested divorce case, and may rebut arguments about abandoning a child or selfishly breaking up a family.

A well written letter of this sort could reduce tensions and actually improve communication with your spouse. However, if you expect to go to court, this is not the time for true confessions. Save candid acknowledgements of your fault in breaking down the marriage, or high praise for your spouse, for another day.

CHAPTER THREE

What Not to Do

Many people are their own worst enemies, especially when in a state of emotional turmoil. The urge to say one more thing, to get the last word, or scratch the itch for immediate revenge, is overwhelming. It feels good at the time, but the price of satisfying that urge can be high.

I once had an informal talk with a potential client in front of his office. Since it was almost lunch time, he kindly bought me a gyro sandwich, bag of chips, and a drink. I clearly remember how great the sandwich smelled, probably because I never got to taste it.

What happened was, my phone rang and I asked him to hold my sandwich. While I was engrossed in the phone call, his wife came up and started talking to him. In a few seconds, the discussion became heated. Then, in a flash and out of the corner of my eye, I saw him push the gyro right down her blouse. There were a few words exchanged. I won't repeat them. Just use your imagination.

Anyway, that was the Pearl Harbor moment of their relationship. Both of them hired lawyers and they went to war, only to resume their normal lives only thousands of dollars and several months later. Would there have been a divorce if my friend hadn't acted out at that moment? Probably. Would it necessary have had to been as prolonged, expensive, and mutually destructive as it eventually became? Almost certainly not. They had only been married a couple of years, were childless, and owned relatively little property.

The point is, anger is a strong motivator. It can make people engage in irrational behavior, and put on blinders to the fact that what they are doing cannot possibly benefit them. Even worse, the effect can linger for a surprisingly long time, like the taste of fish from a long ago meal.

This is worth considering even if your case involves fight to the death issues, and you fully expect to spend a long time in the legal system. Usually, the less your spouse is thinking about you, the dying marriage, and the upcoming appointment with a Judge, the better.

Think of one of the master manipulators of sports, boxer Muhammad Ali. He expended considerable effort, and employed great creativity, in keeping the mind of his opponent off of the one thing that it should have been on, the fight. It was a major reason for his success.

The items on this list are here for another reason too. They are stupid, counterproductive, and can lead to unwanted attention and bad consequences. In divorce litigation, it is relatively easy to create a paper trial that will sink even the sturdiest ship, like a big, unavoidable iceberg bobbing up and down in the water. You can bet that all divorce attorneys, and quite a few divorcing people, are well aware of this.

Having said all that, here is my list. Keep in mind that every situation is unique, so while these rules are sound and solid, they are not invariable.

1. DO NOT involve a new significant other into the dialogue with your estranged spouse. This one should be obvious, but for some reason,

isn't for many people. I once had a client who had a 15 minute divorce hearing to wrap up a case on very favorable terms. He showed up with a new girlfriend half his age clinging tight to his arm, staring the wife down threateningly.

After a few minutes of awkwardness, the hearing commenced. The wife broke down crying, told the Judge that she had made a mistake, and did not want the agreement approved. The fast track divorce became a slow boat to China, to his great detriment.

This rule extends to day to day communication, not just court. Do not put the new boyfriend or girlfriend on the phone to discuss visitation, the credit card bill, or who will be the next American Idol. Some might say that they need a certain comfort level with the ex to allow the new relationship to progress. They are wrong.

2. DO NOT leave the home and children behind, if you want custody.

There are of course some important exceptions to this rule. For openers, if you are temporarily or permanently unable to care properly for them, do not risk a disaster which might forever jeopardize your chances to raise your children. Likewise, if you are in immediate physical danger from your spouse, and satisfied that he or she is not a danger to the children, it might be best to break the rule. However, in such a case, you must act immediately to get the protection you need and set the wheels in motion for a custody hearing. In such situations, you should get an attorney.

Otherwise, there is an unspoken reality to this situation. Thought most judges will deny it, a parent who has been caring for the child(ren) since a separation will probably keep the child(ren), absence neglect or other unusual circumstances. Inertia is among the most powerful forces on earth. If you set up a situation in which the other parent has the opportunity to prove him or herself an at least competent custodial parent, and deprive yourself of the same, the odds on your ultimately winning custody decrease dramatically.

3. DO NOT blame yourself in writing for the breakdown of the marriage.

It is a noble impulse to want to be kind and candid to a loved one at the end of a relationship. It can provide what a therapist would call "closure". It might allow them, and you, to sleep at night.

Remember Leif Garrett? He was a preteen idol in the 1970's, back when I was in high school A few years ago, a "Behind the Music" special was made about him. Turns out that many years ago, on a drunken rampage, he wrecked his car with his best friend along as a passenger. The poor guy was crippled for life, and ended up suing Leif, collecting millions of dollars in compensation.

Not surprisingly, the two best friends lost touch during the litigation and ever after. So to produce a compelling TV moment, the producer arranged for a reunion, with the poor, wheelchair bound injury victim asking in a bewildered tone, "Why did you abandon me?"

Make them a married couple, and make this a conversation about why you left the marital home. If you take the Leif Garrett approach, and spill out your grief, guilt, and regret, you are the same as signing a check that will be cashed in family court.

The attorney representing your husband or wife will present the letter, e mail or text as Exhibit 1 for Plaintiff. The Judge will probably give you a knowing glance followed by a long stare. Your life, and particularly your financial situation, will change.

While matters such as alimony, division of property, and child support are major issues, save such thoughts for a therapist, priest, or trusted confidant to whom you are not married. If you fail to do so, you are sure to regret it later.

When the bullets have been fired, and the court has ruled, you can then seek closure.

4. DO NOT get busy on social media sites, posting photographs and narratives about your new lifestyle. The reasons for this are the same as my reason for recommendation number three. Other than collecting a retainer, the first thing every attorney does is to check these sites to see whether the adverse party is a member, then read and print all of the postings.

As you probably know, but might fail to consider, posting on Face book, Twitter, etc. is about as private as putting up billboards on multiple sites in your hometown, except that at least the billboard will be taken down in a few weeks. The internet postings are there forever.

A good rule for life, and especially for someone involved in divorce or custody litigation, is to ask you before posting, "is what I am saying something that I would be comfortable with everybody knowing about me?" Unless the answer is an unhesitating "No," then DON'T DO IT.

5. DO NOT meet with the estranged husband or wife in private places or alone. The current state of law enforcement procedure in most jurisdictions is that if there is an allegation of domestic violence, or even an allegation of a threat, the police take the supposed culprit into custody. Of course, he or she will have a day in court later. However, that date might come well after he or she has lost a job, lost the right to possess a firearm, been subject to a family court restraining order, and suffered all sorts of other punitive consequences due to the accusation.

There is a real difficulty in the minds of most people in deciding how much to trust a recently estranged husband or wife. On one hand, this is a person with whom they have shared a life, dreams, ambitions, and possibly children. This involves intimacy and ideally, absolute trust. One the other hand, this is now a person who has a directly adversarial role to them, strong motivation to hurt them, and an equally conflicted and possibly unstable emotional response to them.

The law is heavily skewed towards preventing domestic violence. Consequentially, after the fact is far too late to prove that you are not an abusive spouse. Instead of meeting in the home privately, suggest meeting in a public place where you can expect a crowd, such as a restaurant or a shopping mall. If the circumstances dictate that you must go to the home, or another less than ideal place, bring along someone you trust, such as a close friend or family member.

6. DO NOT cut off communication with your ex. This sounds a little contradictory at first. It is absolutely true that you now need to get in the habit, at least in the short term, of keeping your private life private. However, anything you can find out about the activities, plans, or thoughts of your spouse is going to be to your benefit. Think of it as something along the lines of military intelligence.

The conversations can often be unpleasant, stressful, and even scary. Still, in the worst scenario, if your ex was thinking "I am going to buy a gun and kill you!" wouldn't you want to know that?

Try your best to be a good, active listener. This might even facilitate a peaceful and sane resolution to your problems. If not, it will at least give you insight into the thoughts, plans, and intentions of your enemy.

7. DO NOT cut off support for your child(ren), especially if you have any intent to pursue custody or joint custody.

If your child(ren) is/are in the primary custody of your spouse, there are only three things you can do to show the court that you are an interested and capable parent. The first is to exercise as much visitation with the child (ren) as possible. The second is to pursue your legal rights to custody or visitation promptly and aggressively. The third is to support the child(ren) financially.

Even if your spouse is well able to afford the bills without your help, failure to pay support is typically seen as abandonment. If there is no court order, the support can take the form of providing needed items for the child, but keep records and receipts of all such expenditures. Frequently, the payment of voluntary support by a non custodial parent will be denied under oath, unless there is a paper trail. Even if you are not a good record keeper, get in the habit of documenting these expenditures.

8. DO NOT voluntarily pay more in support than you can afford in the long run. The problem with this is the probability that, shown evidence of what amount you have voluntarily paid, a trial judge will

consider this as a bottom line in setting up your permanent child support or alimony obligation, working up from there. This would mean that your short term generosity would be permanent and enforceable by court order, with the possibility of jail time if not paid.

For the same reason, it is usually a poor idea to leave the former marital home if you want possession in the long run. This is especially true if you consider yourself unlikely, due to your income or credit rating, to be able to obtain suitable alternative housing easily. Particularly where the is a substantial mortgage on the house, the court is unlikely to order you to continue paying the mortgage, taxes, and other household expenses if you do not live there. However, by abandoning the house, you are at a minimum sending the message that you are willing to leave your spouse in possession. If this is not the case, doing so is a bad idea.

9. DO NOT tell your spouse that you know about an affair or other conduct that you plan to use in court. Unless you are completely satisfied, and your lawyer is as well, that you have sufficient proof, this is the best favor you can do for them. If your spouse cares anything about the results of the pending family court action, they will either end the adulterous

relationship, or at least become much more secretive about their conduct, making it easier to deny the fact in court.

10. DO NOT threaten or attempt to intimidate your spouse, especially in writing. No explanation is really needed here. However, this extends not only to violence. If you intend to play hardball in the litigation, or want to punish your spouse in some way, avoid the urge to express this thought, especially in writing. Any such statement can be used against you in court. If you are not quite up to forgiveness at the moment, keep in mind another expression. "Revenge is a dish best served cold."

11. DO NOT leave irreplaceable personal items with your spouse if you leave the marital home. .

I have often seen the destruction of family photos, wedding dresses, furniture that had been in a family for generations, and other such items. In every case, we were able to get compensation in trial, often exceeding the value of the item, but the thing itself was irreplaceable. It was scarcely a comfort to the client. This really makes sense. After all, what better way to attack a person who in your mind abandoned you than to destroy the things that define him or her?

12. DO NOT reconcile with a suddenly remorseful spouse who has just been caught red handed. It is not my purpose to discourage married couples from saving their marriages. Still, an offer of reconciliation in some circumstances has to be looked upon as a Trojan horse.

Where there is a great deal at stake, and it becomes suddenly clear that you have a strong likelihood of success in court, this can change the attitude of your estranged. However, the reasons might be more tactical than emotional. Unless there is some real indication that he or she sincerely wants to work on the problems which caused the breakdown of the marriage, there is little hope of saving it.

If, for whatever reason, you sincerely wish to save the marriage, suggest that the two of you spend more time together, date, or pursue counseling. However, speak to your attorney about what consequences might result from a reconciliation of even a brief nature. When in doubt, allow the head to overrule the heart, at least for a time.

CHAPTER FOUR

Good Habits make for good results

After the first couple of days, life may be reverting at least somewhat back to normal. Whether or not this is the case, you are left with the uncertainty of a pending divorce action, which might last months, or years, with a consequentially unstable personal and financial life. While none of this works towards improving your short term quality of life, there are things you can do to restore some sanity and stability.

First of all, give careful thought and consideration to what you will tell friends and family about the situation. If there is still some civility and trust with your spouse, discuss this issue with him or her. This is a good idea for several reasons.

By doing so, you express concern and respect for the feelings of your spouse. Many people are more injured by second hand statements heard through the gossip mill then they ever were by anything an estranged spouse ever actually said.

Suggest that the two of you agree to a polite question and answer about the marital situation. For example, a good, safe answer to the question is "Yes, we are involved in a trial separation and working on our relationship." Of course, that response will satisfy few with the curiosity of even a dead cat.

If you are successful, this can be a bridge to a constructive post-separation relationship, albeit a swinging, narrow, and dangerous rope bridge.

It can also prevent, or at least limit, the amount of talk. Whether or not you consider yourself at fault in the breakdown of your marriage, this is to your benefit. It helps keep friends from feeling the pressure to choose sides, or alternately, disassociate from one of both of the parties. This is important whether or not the divorce becomes a contested legal matter.

Either way, it is also important to collect, preserve, and document whatever useful information or potential testimony can be provided, should it be needed later. This can include friendly witness testimony that would build you up as a spouse or parent, testimony that shows your spouse in a negative light as husband, wife or parent, or corroboration of important facts such as proof of adultery, abuse, or neglect of children.

The best way to do this is also the most obvious and cheapest. Have the witness write out a statement by hand, and sign it. This is preferable to a typed statement because the handwriting and signature can be used to prove that the words are indeed those of the person in question, should this be necessary. The signature can also be verified by a notary public.

This modest amount of extra trouble can be priceless when, as is often the case, a witness decides months later that he or she does not wish to be inconvenienced to attend a hearing, or does not want to get caught in the middle of your marital dispute after all. It very simply forces him or her to stick to the truth, and avoids any possibility of "forgetting."

At all costs, however, try to avoid alienating family and friends during this period. Many people will feel pressure to choose sides in the relationship, and disassociate from one or the other of the couple. This is inevitable whether or not the parties do anything to create such pressure. The result is that you will have a short window of opportunity in which you can probably talk to most potential witnesses in the case, after which they will choose alliances and some will refuse to speak with you.

By not throwing down a gauntlet, you will have a better opportunity to speak with them freely, collect information you need, and also create or preserve goodwill. If you want their cooperation as a potential witness, explain to them that the more information you have now, the better the chance of avoiding the need for deposition or trial testimony. If they refuse to write out a statement, be skeptical as to whether they can be counted on at trial.

Also, from this point on, keep copies of all communications with your spouse in any form, including e mails, texts, and voice mails. Regularly check any and all social media of which he or she is a member, and print any pages that might later be significant.

It is also a good time to learn a few good habits as to dealing with your spouse. These can keep minor arguments from the coming major disputes, and a long way towards maintaining sanity and stability.

It all possible, try not to respond to text, e-mails, or voice mails when you are angry. Depending on your mental state, it is a good idea to wait between one hour and one day to respond to a communication which you consider insulting, inflammatory, or threatening. In reality, it might not always be possible to do this. However, it is least always possible to exhale, take a moment, and then think the situation through before acting.

In doing this, keep in mind that practically all communication now can be documented and preserved, thus making anything a potential trial exhibit. Like anyone else, judges and juries tend to dislike people who are angry, bitter, and irrational. By contrast, they much prefer people who keep their cool, and focus on the big picture, such as protecting their children.

The momentary satisfaction of returning a verbal slap in the face with like kind treatment is not worth the long-term damage. Every action you take should be consistent with furthering your agenda as to how the contested matters in your case should be resolved. Keeping this in mind, it is much easier to keep your cool.

This is also the time to engage in information gathering, especially if children are involved. There are many essential documents that might be needed on short notice for various reasons, including school records, medical records, and financial statements. All are difficult to obtain quickly. There are several reasons for this, not the least of them the fact that large corporations are increasingly less attuned to the needs of a customer absent a strong profit motive.

Usually, their lightening fast capacity to post a bill is not equaled by their ability to respond to other requests. To be fair, this sometimes has to do with privacy concerns. Nevertheless, it is wise to collect whatever information you might need as soon as you become aware of it. The availability can sometimes be completely lost, such as with the medical records of a spouse. Even if not, few entities will accommodate an urgent need that does not directly benefit them.

How does one determine what documents he or she might need? The question can easily be answered once you are able to answer the question "What facts do I need to prove if my case goes to trial?" Sometimes, these questions are best answered by an attorney. Usually, however, a non lawyer can reason these issues through and come up with pretty accurate ideas.

For example, if you are seeking to prove adultery, and get your hands on a phone bill that documents your spouse's calls, you have gold. Likewise, if the competence of your spouse as a parent is limited due to a drug or alcohol problem, medical records and counseling records might constitute definitive proof, but are difficult to obtain. Want to prove who made the house payments for all those years? The bank statements and credit card records are essential.

If you carefully go through this process, you can save big money in attorney's fees, and dramatically increases your chances of success in court. Remember that the closer you get to a court date, the more reluctant potential witnesses will be to cooperate, and the more problematic slow responses to requests for documents will be.

With that in mind, here is a list of some of the more typical trial issues, and items of evidence which, if available, are relevant to proving important facts.

1. Adultery: ANY communication in any form between the spouse and the paramour. This would include telephone records, e mail, text messages, photographs, social media postings, cards, letters, etc. Also, any communication to yourself, or a third party, which makes reference to the affair, can be crucial evidence. Credit Card, Bank Accounts, and checking account records can provide solid proof of the whereabouts of an individual at a given time, making it relatively simple to follow the footprints.

Keep in mind that there are state and federal laws that prohibit wiretapping and other illicit tracking of others, including a spouse. Due to the rapid improvement in the technologies that allow for this, and an equally rapid decrease in the price, more and more people are tempted to go this route. The law in most states is well behind in providing a mechanism for enforcement of the law in this area, but the laws do exist on the books. Do not attempt to guess the password of your spouse and hack into a telephone, computer, or other device, unless you are willing to risk serious consequences.

2. Abuse of drugs or alcohol: The best evidence, of course, would be a charge or conviction for a substance abuse related crime. The proof is usually a matter of public record, and can be obtained by a web search, or a phone call to the courthouse. Otherwise, photographs or home video can speak a thousand words about the condition, or fitness, of an individual. Check social web sites for party pictures, which many people habitually post.

3. Physical Abuse: Unfortunately, the best evidence here might well be your own medical records, or pictures. A prior criminal history is highly probative and will make any impression on any judge. If there is a

criminal prosecution, the incident report court transcripts, and of course, proof of conviction are essential.

    4. Contributions to Marital Property: Financial records, especially checking account statements and credit card statements, can be definitive if the parties maintain separate accounts. As to non monetary contributions, witness testimony is often the best evidence. However, photographs and video can document things like improvements to the home and yard, etc.

    5. Ownership of Property: Credit card statements, bank statements, and receipts can be the best evidence of who provided the purchase money to acquire an item. Otherwise, it can be difficult to determine precisely who owns what, with the issue usually determined by the testimony of witnesses.

    6. Responsibility for Debts: See the responses to numbers four and five above.

    7. Entitlement to Custody or Visitation with a Child: The first and best source for support is with caregivers outside of the immediate family. This would include doctors who treat the child, school teachers or day care employees, and the like. If they are willing to do so, these individuals

can speak about the relationship of the child with a parent, and the extent of involvement of a parent in the child's day to day activities, as well as the overall health, well being, and happiness of the child. These are the individuals who should be approached first in a contested custody case.

If these sources are not cooperative, or readily available, look inward. Photographs of parent and child together, handwritten notes or drawings by the child, holiday videos and the like can be very powerful statements in court. Also, do not make the mistake of disregarding the testimony of friendly witnesses including family members. While their motives might be subject to challenge due to their loyalty to you, it is undeniable that those with the closest bonds to the family will observe the most, and thus, have the most complete story to tell.

8. Expert Witnesses: We live in a time when great weight is given to experts, even if their credentials are often exaggerated, their opinions biased, and their expertise often self proclaimed. If enough is at issue, you might have to consider budgeting for an expert as to any of the issues noted herein. However, it might well be that your expert is already available to you, due to an ongoing business or personal relationship. This

can include your treating physician, your banker, a school counselor or teacher, or a party serving your spouse in any of these categories.

After reviewing this list, you should be able to identify the issues which you would want to prove in a trial. You should also be able to pinpoint the types of evidence which need to be collected to achieve your goal. All that remains is to follow up in gathering the necessary items, or document the testimony of the witnesses in question.

The next issue to resolve is whether you choose to do this yourself, or to hire an attorney to do it for you.

CHAPTER FIVE

The Hired Gun.

From day one in the process, you probably already have a strong inclination as to whether you would want to hire an attorney. As a general rule, the greater the number of times you have had to deal with attorneys in the past, for whatever reason, the better your understanding of whether you need one in a particular situation.

There are two common mistakes I see people make as to this issue. The first is to act without legal advice in a complex, contested situation, making catastrophic and often irrevocable mistakes. The second is to hire an attorney in a situation where relatively little is at stake and due to poor judgment, or possibly the machinations of the attorney, run up a large, completely unnecessary legal bill.

Once you decide that you need one, it is equally problematic to pick the shoe that fits. In other words, how much expertise and how high a billable rate suit your purposes? The following is a series of questions designed to help you answer the question, with a scaled points system.

1. Are you seeking custody of your child? This point must be thought through now, in a calm, clearheaded way. If you are satisfied that your spouse is a good parent, and concede that he or she is the principle caregiver, proceed carefully. Then ask yourself if you are truly comfortable with the life adjustments necessary to raise a child of whatever age, possibly without significant help. If revenge or getting the last word is a

primary motive, know that the joy of revenge fades quickly, but the responsibilities outlast it by far.

If, on the other hand, you are the primary caregiver for your child, the answer is obvious. This is even more important where the other parent is unfit due to neglect or abuse. Whatever the reason, if the answer is yes: ADD FIVE POINTS.

2. Does the net value of the marital property justify the expense of attorney fees? While there can be no set formula to answer this question, here are a few generally applicable rules. First of all, if the net worth of the marital property is under ten thousand dollars, this argues strongly against hiring an attorney. (Net property, by way of definition, means the value of the items you own minus any debt attached to them. In other words, if you own a hundred thousand dollar house with a ninety thousand dollar mortgage, you have a ten thousand dollar asset, not a hundred thousand dollar asset.) At below ten thousand dollars in assets, you could win all of the property at trial, and still spend more on attorney fees than the value of your "victory."

If the value is greater, the question is more complex. If you have a relatively strong, undamaged degree of trust in your spouse, and can arrange a settlement, this will probably save you money. However, you must keep in mind that no settlement is enforceable in the law until approved in court by a judge. Until then, you are relying on the good faith of your partner to not dispose of, destroy, mortgage, or otherwise squander your share of the marital property. This is a risky judgment call to make. Consider the possible effects of a breach of the agreement, and figure the risk in making your decision.

If the net value of the property is above ten thousand dollars, and there is no chance of a fair settlement at this early stage, you might well need an attorney. A good formula for deciding whether to hire an attorney, and especially to hire a particular attorney, is to avoid spending any more than one dollar in attorney fees to every four dollars of value in the marital estate, unless there are other issues that must be litigated, such as child custody or support.

If the marital estate is of sufficient value to suggest that you need an attorney, ADD THREE POINTS.

3. Are you, or is your spouse, seeking any kind of permanent support, such as alimony, rehabilitative alimony, or permanent payment of health care premiums?

If so, ADD THREE POINTS.

4. Are you, or your spouse, seeking to prove fault based divorce grounds, such as adultery, habitual drunkenness, or physical cruelty? If so, are the allegations being used as a basis to obtain other relief, such as an increased share of marital property, custody of a child, support, or attorney fees?

If so, ADD THREE POINTS.

5. If you have a child, and are not seeking custody, is your spouse making it difficult for you to communicate with and visit with your child? Is the child being alienated from you by the words and actions of your spouse? Is the child being used as "bait" when the custodial parent wants money, needs a baby sitter, or has some other motive?

If so, ADD FIVE POINTS.

6. Have you been left paying bills which, in your opinion, are rightly the responsibility of your spouse? This would include debt for items which are retained and possessed by him or her, and/or uniquely for his or her purposes. If so, does the spouse have the financial capacity to pay these bills, despite his or her refusal to do so?

If so, ADD THREE POINTS.

7. Has your spouse threatened you with violence, taken actions which did, or could have resulted in a charge of criminal domestic violence, or acted in a fashion that made you genuinely afraid.

If so, ADD THREE POINTS.

8. Are you financially dependent upon your spouse? If so, are you without immediate marketable skills or financial assets which would allow you to survive without his or her support?

If so, ADD FIVE POINTS.

9. Are you immediately concerned about the possibility that your spouse might leave your home, taking your child(ren), property, or savings?

If so, ADD FIVE POINTS.

10. Are you comfortable with the idea of participating in a contested divorce action? To determine this, reflect on your overall feelings about confrontation. For example, do you enjoy going to a car lot and haggling with a salesman over price? Have you ever represented yourself in a minor legal matter, such as a traffic ticket?

I mention this for a reason. Few people consider the psychological effects of being involved in a contested legal matter on their quality of life before choosing to get involved. These cases can literally drag on for years. For many, the result is severe anxiety, depression, and countless sleepless nights. If your heart beat races at the thought of going to court, for your own sake, carefully consider other options.

If this is not an issue for you, ADD FIVE POINTS.

The test can be scored as follows:

If you score thirty to forty points (30-40), you need to hire an attorney.

If you score twenty to twenty nine points (20-29), you would benefit by hiring an attorney, but might be able to resolve your issues without counsel. If you choose to do so, proceed with caution and obtain legal counsel immediately if you sense that you are in over your head.

If you score ten to nineteen points (10-19), you still would benefit by hiring an attorney, but should be very cost conscious about the decision.

If you score zero to nine points (0-9), you would only need an attorney if you are uncomfortable or unable to file the papers for a simple divorce in your state without the assistance of counsel. The process, of course, varies from state to state. I would suggest contacting your State Bar, the local Clerk of Court, or a neighborhood legal assistance program for more information.

The next question, of course, is how do I find the attorney best suited to my needs? Finding the answer is a lot like searching for water with a divining rod. Sometimes, you just have to get lucky.

The main reason for this is the essential nature of the attorney-client relationship. Simply put, the effectiveness of the attorney can only be determined in context of his or her ability to work with the client as a team. In other words, a well seasoned, highly competent attorney who knows all there is to know about your kind of case might be a very poor choice for you. It is really a question of temperament, priorities and goals.

There are a few constants of which you should be aware. First of all, the priciest is very often not the best. Like any other product, legal services can be packaged in the trappings of success, expensive offices, thick carpet, antique furniture, etc. to give an appearance of additional value. Often, this is enough to convince potential clients that the apparent prestige and success of the firm will translate into success. The two do not necessarily correlate.

Particularly if you have limited issues in your case, such as a moderate amount of marital property to divide and possibly some debts, a high cost law firm makes absolutely no sense. This is for the same reason you would not invest one hundred dollars in an attempt to win fifty dollars.

Even if you do have serious issues which justify the costs, look beyond the trappings and ask hard questions about the firm or attorney. The questions should not be directed at the attorney or firm employees, who will simply parrot out their sales pitch. Instead, talk to former clients of the firm if possible, other attorneys, or friends with ties in the legal profession.

Also, do not assume that an apparently well connected attorney can influence a judge inappropriately. Such things do happen, but not as often as you might believe. Few cases are of a value that would convince a Judge to risk his or her reputation, career, and pension by engaging in seriously unethical conduct.

If you do go this route, pay careful attention to the retainer agreement. Despite what you will be told, everything in the contract is negotiable, particularly in this economy. Try to negotiate a reduction in the billable hours rate, as well as (and this is crucial) a ceiling as to the total amount of the attorney fees. Without this, the probability is that the attorney will simply pad the billable hours to make up for the reduction in the hourly rate.

On the other end of the spectrum, you do want an attorney with adequate experience to handle the case with confidence. I would normally suggest that you be reluctant to hire an attorney who has less than three years of experience, unless he or she is supervised. You do not want him or her to get their training while shaping your future life.

Ideally, attempt to find an attorney who has the following qualities:

1. At least three years of experience, with an emphasis in the family law field.

2. A clean ethical record. (This can be confirmed through a simple inquiry with the state bar.)

3. A reputation of practicing regularly in the county or district in which your

case will be tried. (Notwithstanding what I said earlier, plenty of home cooking occurs in family

court, as it does everywhere else. You don't want to be a victim of this.)

4. Who is willing to negotiate a flat rate fee, or a fee ceiling and reduction on the hourly billable

rate.

5. Who listens to you in the initial consultation, appears to understand your priorities, and

communicates a clear plan as to how to proceed.

You should be asked to sign a written retainer agreement, of which you will be given a copy. Keep this and all other documents from your attorney in the permanent file you will be maintaining throughout the divorce proceedings.

CONCLUSION

If you follow the advice in this book, you will be well prepared for whatever course the future takes. Should there be an opportunity to settle your case, you will be able to negotiate with informed confidence. If the matter is to go to trial, you will have the documentation needed to win.

Like so many other things in life, the only constant in a separation or divorce is change. For that reason, you will need to re-evaluate the situation periodically, to be sure that the decisions you made initially are still sound, and in the best interests of yourself and your family. It might be beneficial to review the questions about child custody, or whether you should retain an attorney, when new facts become know or events occur.

The only thing that should remain constant is your goals, provided that they were carefully thought out at the beginning. If they are based on the right priorities, the rest of your plan can be expected to fall into place.

www.ingramcontent.com/pod-product-compliance
Lightning Source LLC
Chambersburg PA
CBHW071819170526
45167CB00003B/1370